The Biggest Bark

Order this book online at www.trafford.com/08-1091
or email orders@trafford.com

Most Trafford titles are also available at major online book retailers.

Note for Librarians: A cataloguing record for this book is available from Library
and Archives Canada at www.collectionscanada.ca/amicus/index-e.html

Printed in Victoria, BC, Canada.

ISBN: 978-1-4251-4935-2 (sc)

*We at Trafford believe that it is the responsibility of us all, as both individuals
and corporations, to make choices that are environmentally and socially sound.
You, in turn, are supporting this responsible conduct each time you purchase a
Trafford book, or make use of our publishing services. To find out how you are
helping, please visit www.trafford.com/responsiblepublishing.html*

*Our mission is to efficiently provide the world's finest, most comprehensive
book publishing service, enabling every author to experience success.
To find out how to publish your book, your way, and have it available
worldwide, visit us online at www.trafford.com/10510*

Trafford
PUBLISHING   www.trafford.com

North America & international
toll-free: 1 888 232 4444 (USA & Canada)
phone: 250 383 6864 ✦ fax: 250 383 6804 ✦ email: info@trafford.com

The United Kingdom & Europe
phone: +44 (0)1865 487 395 ✦ local rate: 0845 230 9601
facsimile: +44 (0)1865 481 507 ✦ email: info.uk@trafford.com

10 9 8 7 6 5 4

The Biggest Bark

102 Dog Poems

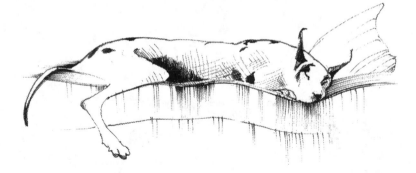

Hugh O'Connell

Title cover and illustrations by Richard O'Connell

This book is dedicated to

Benjamin

of

The Dog's Trust Rehoming Centre,
Evesham, England.

Contents

Dog Sonnet

More than a pet, a loyal friend,
Whose affection has no end.
More than a friend, a guardian,
Who'll defend twenty-four seven.
More than a guard, a helping hand,
Who'll obey every command.
More than a helping hand, a servant,
Who fulfills whatever the need or want.
More than a servant, a partner,
Forever faithful to mistress or master.
More than a partner, becomes a part
Who's found in every owner's heart.
More than a part, almost as one,
And like the moon will follow the sun.

Meals on Heels

Their friends thought it the real deal,
When invited around for an evening meal.

Charlie, the host's beagle puppy,
Played quite happily,
Until he flopped in a heap
Under the dining table for an impromptu sleep.

All went well at the dinner party
Concluding with a chocolate and coffee.

The satisfied guests started to leave -
Under the table one lady retrieved
Her shoes, but after she slipped them on,
She staggered and fell down!

They thought at the time
It was due to an excess of French red wine.
Until they saw both heels
Had been chewed right through,
By, guess who? Charlie the beagle!
Under the table, he was able
To turn expensive heels into a two course meal!

Of course, the bemused beagle,
Believed his 'ground floor meal' quite legal!

Dog Donor Honour

A two-year-old English mastiff has shown
He's one of the kindest dogs ever known.
No better friend could you expect to get
To help save a critically injured pet.

Lurch offers a lifeline night and day,
For which distressed dog owners pray.
Lurch just loves giving blood.
In fact, it flows like a flood.

Twenty separate blood donations
Has exceeded all canine expectations!
The American Red Cross
Honours Lurch's controlled blood loss.

Michigan's Chapter,
As a reward,
Allocates to Lurch
'The 2008 Pets Best Friend Award'.

Fascinating Friendships

Is there no end to whom a dog will befriend ?

Six Siamese kittens
Proved no barrier
To being mothered by Tammy,
A Yorkshire Terrier.

Who would possibly have thought
That Thumper the Leveret,
Would simply adore
Queenie the Labrador ?

Flossie the lamb, without a qualm,
Fell for a Belgian Shepherd.

Roxanne the Rottweiler
Frightened many a man,
But proved gentle and calm
With fifteen goats on a farm.

Three new born leopard cubs
Were a formidable club,
But were neither a hindrance or a hitch
To Deese, the mongrel bitch.

Two baby deer felt no fear
When a Pointer named Diana came near.
She was treated like no other
As if their long lost mother!

Mickey the tame mouse found
Friendship with sanguine Saffron,
A benevolent bloodhound.

Two unique bedfellows -
A dog and a cockerel.
They confirm fur and feathers
Co-exist extremely well !

A sheep dog called Coquette
Felt she'd found the perfect pets,
When she adopted two orphan piglets.

Wooster, a cross breed Dalmatian,
Was locally known as
'The Dog who Loved the Cat Shelter'.
(But never allowed pussy near her bone!)

Three tiger cubs did not deter Bessie,
The black Collie,
Who gave them a feed whenever needed.

But the greatest surprise
Of dog friendships lies
With a pup who got lost.
Until a vixen adopted the Collie cross,
(Some say she stole it!)
But kept it fed and safe from the cold,
Deep inside her fox hole.

Honey and Cheese

There's something a bit funny
About an Alsatian cross called Honey.

His bark is loud and clear,
Whenever he thinks danger near.

He loves chasing a frisbee anywhere,
Whenever it sails through the air !

But, basically, Honey's a real softee.
Soft mints melt his heart instantly.

Wet weather walks ? Don't bother!
Honey decides instead to go to bed!

He'll also do whatever you please
In exchange for a piece of cheese !

Max

I know that white fluffy face,
    Full of Westie pride,
As he ambles through the village
    With Doris by his side.

Not once, nor twice,
    But three times they stroll a day,
Over the little bridges
    Where Max watches children play.

I know that little wagging tail
    Along path, track or lane,
Where Max is taken for walks,
    Not once but again and again!

He's getting on in doggie years,
    Now all of fourteen;
And needs a daily cooked diet
    To keep him fit and lean!

I know Max loves everyone
    He meets when walking around.
His behaviour has earned Heaven,
    He'll reach in one bound !

Jane and Whiskey in the Back Room

To earn pocket money
    Jane worked in a greasy cafe,
Serving cheap, fattening meals
    Which sickened her every day.

Then Jane discovered
    In a small, dim, back room
A little terrier tied to a chair.
    His face riddled in gloom.

His name was Whiskey
    And since a pup he was kept
Chained like a prisoner
    To that chair day and night.

For meals Whiskey was pelted
    With scraps left on a plate.
Jane was appalled at such cruelty
    And triggered a kinder fate!

She fell in love with the little dog
    Which proved his salvation,
For the owners openly admitted
    They'd prefer a big Alsatian!

Whiskey was due to be put down,
    So Jane immediately offered
To buy Whiskey, by paying weekly
    From her wages for his liberty.

She gave Whiskey good food
    And a ball to learn how to play,
Until the great day arrived
    When Jane led him from the cafe.

She could not afford a lead,
    So used a length of washing line.
He'd never seen the sky
    Nor smelt fresh green grass!

Into a meadow she let Whiskey go,
    Where he ran amok among
Grass, trees, wildflowers, bushes
    And birds in full, joyful song!

Despite his weak back legs
    And a low back due to cowering,
Whiskey could not stop
    Running, leaping and rolling!

He leapt and chased dragon flies
    And sniffed daisy and buttercup !
Transformed into a bundle of joy
    Like any delighted, new-born pup !

Nightmare on Farm Street

Jodie, the farm Collie, counted sheep
In order to obtain a well-earned sleep,
But at a considerable cost
For if a lamb got lost,
He'd wake from slumber with a leap!

Buried Alive

Percy the Chihuahua was run over by a car.
Pa put Percy in a sack and buried him
In a shallow grave in the back garden.

No one grieved more than his best friend,
Mickey, the family's adorable Labrador.

But that same night,
Pa awoke to sounds from the garden,
Full heart felt whining and scuffling!

When Pa looked out of the window
He saw Mickey had dug up the grave,
Ripped open the sack, and was giving Percy
The 'kiss of life' - as if he could be saved!
Such was Mickey's grief for his little friend,
He was unwilling to admit
Percy's life had come to an end.

Pa went into the garden and stooped down -
Next to Mickey engulfed by grief.
But, then, heard Percy give a tiny whimper
To Pa's utter disbelief!
Unbelievably, Percy was still alive,
And in the shallow grave had survived!

For the rescue, Mickey received a reward -
Pro-dog's 'Pet of the Year Award'.

Smoking Kills Pets

Every dog should live in fear
With a smoking owner near.

Canine nasal passages allow
Cancer in their lungs to grow.

It makes them short of breath
And leads to 'walkies with death'.

Bootsie

A story which roused wide compassion
For a little dog who made the news,
Abandoned at Charring Cross Station,
And left to guard an old pair of shoes.

No one dared approach him
As he defended the property of his owner,
Whose return, unbeknown to him, was slim,
For the police suspected he'd done a runner.

The police decided to expand their role
To catch the cast off dog before she roamed,
With a noose at the end of a very long pole
And, then, on to Battersea Dogs Home.

When his plight was nationally shown
In the centre pages of 'The Daily Mirror',
That triggered such a ringing of the phone
From folk wanting to be Bootsie's new owner.

They chose a hairdresser from Bristol,
Who worked in the shop beneath her flat.
So Bootsie was with her night and day
And often the topic of customers' chit chat!

Pooch with a Pouch!

The Labrador pup was traded by its owner
For work Steve completed on his chimney.
But, at home, Sammy proved a pain,
Chasing every duck he could see!
So much so, Steve's wife sent Sammy
To work with her husband every day.
Sammy laid around getting depressed
For he found he could neither work nor play.
Until, one of the roofers hit his thumb,
And threw the hammer into the wood!
Sammy suddenly dashed from the porch -
Believing he was doing what he should -
By chasing after the far flung tool!
Sammy came back clutching the hammer
And climbed up the ladder.
He gladly give it back to the stunned roofer!
From that act his new career reached the news
As the 'Pooch with a Pouch' -
Carrying nails, caps, rivets, plates and screws!
Sammy proved no slouch,
Relishing his job as if carved by fate
As the 'four-legged roofer's mate'.
No better chum, no better gofer,
Had served Sammy's master, also a roofer.
But far away and the best,
Was that Sammy was great for business,
Becoming a celebrity of sorts
In Pembroke, Massachusetts.
During long shifts, Sammy's no longer a loner,
And given doggy treats by a host of home owners.

The Biggest Bark

The competition for 'The Biggest Bark'
Took place in London's Regent's Park.
Dogs came from near and far,
From Walsall to Wales, Shetlands to Shropshire.

There arrived all kinds of doggy breeds,
Pulled along by scores of leads.
Dogs galore crammed the park
To find who could produce the Biggest Bark!

The event was covered by TV and the press
And opened by a 'pooch-loving' celebrity guest!
There was only one test -
To find which dog could bark the best!

Onto the centre of the stage each dog was led
And given one chance to bark off his head.
This proved far from perfect
As it often produced the opposite effect.

A big dog was expected to win again,
But look what happened!
An Alsatian sauntered on and wagged its tail,
But when prompted to bark - failed!

The St. Bernard defied survival laws
And yawned as if completely bored!
Worse was to come from a Labrador,
Who just stared down at the stage floor!

A bulldog ambled on and defiantly glared
At the judges who coldly stared.
A golden retriever was about to bark,
But then sighed at the crowd in the park.

Nor did the flowing Afghan hound
Produce one solitary sound.
A bright eyed greyhound look quite fazed
And gazed around as if in a daze.

A Westie appeared, as pretty as can be,
But then decided to have a little wee.
A spaniel ran on and then ran off,
When one of the judges suddenly coughed.

Some breeds did a little better,
Especially a shimmering Irish Red Setter.
But its bark was deemed insufficient proof,
As it was declared more like a woof!

A Collie stopped dead in the centre
But only snapped as trained by its mentor.
Small dogs like the Pekinese,
Simply yapped, expecting to please.

A poodle did a Number One in full view,
Which even received a cheer or two!
Terriers tried so hard to bark
But were barely heard at the back of the park.

A Jack Russell got quite excitable
But its battery of barks proved unacceptable.
It seemed things were not going to plan
But with animals and children, what can ?

It was, then, on the stage stepped Mel
With Freddie, her four year old mongrel!
When Freddie saw the waiting crowd
He gave a bark so big and loud!

To the rest of the dogs Freddie's bark
Acted like a wake up alarm in the park!
Suddenly, hundreds of dogs on tether,
Began to bark altogether!

Their barking was heard all over the place
And curtains twitched in Buckingham Palace!
Freddie was awarded first prize
For the Biggest Bark of any dog alive!

Mel gave Freddie a great big kiss,
Which to him was truly utter bliss.
Though the reason was well hid,
Why Freddie barked as well as he did -

The crowd reminded Freddie of his old pen
And strangers passing now and again.
It was there the BIGGEST BARK
Freddie learned when he was alone,
Waiting to be adopted in a dog's home.

Extreme Dog Sense

His dog wouldn't dive off the cliff fearing disaster,
Even in the pursuit of his 'extreme sports' master.
So he stood at the top
And barked quite a lot,
While his death-wish owner fell faster and faster!

Insane on the Seine

A dog's devoted stature
Dwarfs man's cruel nature.

From a rowing boat, a young man
Suddenly hurled his dog into the Seine!
His master was trying to drown
A dog he no longer wanted to own!

But the dog struggled back on board,
And was duly chucked back in as a reward.
Twice again the dog climbed on.
But, then, his owner stumbled and fell in!

Onboard the dog would not remain,
And immediately jumped back into the Seine.
To rescue the very man gasping for breath,
Who'd tried to cause its death!

Onto his dog the desperate owner clung,
Until safely rescued by a good samaritan.

What happened next we don't know,
But hope another samaritan also rescued
Our four-legged hero!

The Dog Man of the Imperial Court

Permit me to male my brief report -
I am the Dog Man of the Court.

I clean up Lulu's pee.
But who is Lulu, you may ask,
Who offloads onto me
Such a thankless task ?

Lulu is the lapdog who's always near
His Most Exceptional
And Extraordinary Majesty,
Haile Selassie, Emperor of Ethiopia.

My purpose sure and certain
To carry a satin napkin,
For cleaning VIP shoes
If Lulu urinates on them.

Yet Lulu will only wee
To mark out new territory.
It's her way of giving her blessing,
After she's done some 'sniff testing'.

No one passes a critical word
Whether ambassador or lord,
Minister or Consulate,
Governor or Directorate.

I quickly stoop
Where Lulu had widdled or pooped,
And, within ten seconds time,
Spattered shoes once more shine!

Lulu's reputation among diplomats
Is worse than kitchen rats!
If it wasn't for the King,
Lulu's little neck they'd readily wring!

VIPs secretly deem her rude
And insufferably crude.
Protocol forbids adverse reactions,
Even a frown can provoke sanctions.

Lulu's waterworks
Can drive dignitaries quietly berserk.
So I am often urgently sought
As Dog Man of the Imperial Court.

And remain aloof as I,
Once more,
Stoop before a glittering group
With my satin cloth, spray and scoop.

Collie I.Q. Rules, OK?

How can it possibly get any better
For an Irish Red Setter ?
Flowing russet coat, eyes nut brown,
Totally disarms with charm.

But such views cannot alter the result,
Most dogs consider an insult !
From thousands genuinely appalled,
Here are a few who called:

Bulldogs grunted, spaniels snapped,
Huskies howled,
Terriers snarled, Rottweilers barked,
Mongrels growled!

Only collies kept sane
Having, officially, the Best Dog Brain.
Red Setters also envy their coat -
The colours of Ireland's most notable stout !

Maternal Mongrels

The pups of Pip Martin Royle
Were found new homes countryside.
So, she then took charge
Of the family's youngest child.

Turning over the baby
When needing a nappy, and if crying
Allowing no one near the pram,
Unless it was her mother approaching.

Poodle Loverock watched
Children playing outside near the park,
And if anyone whimpered,
He alerted their mothers with a bark.

The mistress of Scatty Weatherill
Tied her baby's reins to his dog collar,
And the dog taught him
To beware of any lorry, bus or car.

Kim Hurst helped Gran
By rocking her grandson in the pram.
While Tramp, took to the sea,
To ensure her grandson paddled safely.

Just a few examples to demonstrate
Why Mongrels are so great.
Indeed, only the very, very best
Win parents' trust.

Kennel Heaven

Good dogs need never fear,
    As the Holy Book makes clear.

After all, it was people - not nice -
    First slung out of Paradise.

Animals remained, unlike men,
    Inside the Garden of Eden.

But is it really so very odd,
    For Dog re-coded is 'God' ?

So, ergo, Dog Heaven
    Offered twenty four seven.

What did Mongrels do in the War ?

Can't you see, can't you tell,
From faded photos in black and white?
I was the soldiers' mongrel,
Standing before, by and after the fight!

Sometimes I was the star,
Wearing a tin helmet at a rakish angle
Or a working dog of war,
Wearing an ammo belt like a bangle.

Ratting, a real task,
Among mud-filled, towering trenches.
I often wore a gas mask
And the loss of my friends still wrenches.
Sometimes I'd merrily go
To bombed out places,
Where you'll see me sitting on an old piano,
Howling beside plucky faces.

I sailed on submarines and battleships
Wearing a sailor's hat;
And performed all sorts of party tricks,
Unless chasing a rat!

Sometimes I'd sit on an airstrip
Or a jungle track,
Waiting week after week
For my master who was never coming back.

9/11 Rescue Dogs

The Best Noses and the Biggest Hearts
in the world were summoned on 9/11.

Over 350 dogs were involved -
Labrador Retrievers, Golden Retrievers,
German Shepherds, Collies, Rottweilers
and scores of other dogs.

Two guide dogs led their blind owners
Down seventy smoke filled floors.

The first purpose of the rescue dog:
to seek and find Life. In return, a reward,
such as a soft ball or toy or verbal praise.
They worked side by side with their handlers,
sharing their risks of bodily injury
and exposure to known and unknown toxins.

Broken glass, sharp debris, twisted metal,
could pierce their eyes, paws, arteries.
Every breath and every step potentially fatal
They willingly penetrated the twin abyss
of foul-smelling, smoke-filled, smouldering,
treacherous cavities, holes, pits, tunnels, voids.

Dogs were hoisted and lowered on cradles
to search areas to dangerous for handlers.

This was their territory and the duty

they had been trained for -
to detect body sweat and stress odours.

They sniffed and scoured in pitch darkness,
crawled on their bellies to overcome
the mega-minefields that infested titanic debris.

Their delight matched by their handlers,
whenever they detected a survivor.

Dog teams worked around the clock,
putting in gruelling 12 to 16 hour shifts.

Dogs also provided wry amusement
for exhausted, overwhelmed workers.
One Golden Labrador walked around
holding his handler's helmet in his mouth.

Dogs comforted those in shock
to traumatised to express their feelings.

Yet, nothing rivalled the terrible task
of finding those who did not survive.

As the long, demanding days wore on,
some rescue dogs became depressed,
as if believing it was their fault for not finding
more survivors as the body count soared.

So their handlers arranged 'mock finds',
where fire-fighters 'hid' in the rubble
and the dogs would be sent to 'find' them.

This strategy restored the dogs' spirits
and they would return refreshed for work.

Aware of their critical importance,
a canine medical team was also on site
to treat them for injuries and exhaustion.

9/11 rescue dogs were, without exception,

The Canine Heroes of Ground Zero

Ancient War Dogs

The Victories of War Dogs learn:
The Garamantes king held his throne,
Supported by two hundred dogs.
The Colophonians and Castabalians
Cohorts of dogs, prized above cattle,
Displayed valour matching centurions',
And never surrendered in battle.

Our breastplates and spiked collars
Ward off spears, swords and arrows.
In the hearts of the bravest soldiers,
Fear arises on hearing our howls.
We are War Dogs with a vice-like bite
And guard our camp day and night.
Intruders we'll rip apart on sight
And love nothing better than a fight.

We're trained to attack and obey
Whatever the hour, whatever the day.
We gladly follow our masters into war
For we're the Frontline Dog Corps.
And when released from our chain,
We're keen to inflict the greatest pain.
So we growl and snarl, snap and roar,
And relish the enemy between our jaws!

The Celts led dog regiments into war,
Ferocious, fearless, whatever the call.
Battalions trained dog driven corps,
Kept as bodyguards to Kings of Gaul.
In the Middle Ages horses feared
War dogs wearing fitted breastplates,
Razor sharp scythes and fire goblets.
Their canine hearts stoked with hate.

Our collars, studded with spikes,
Will rip open armoured leg and arm.
Even the battle ground shakes
When dog brigades bark warning alarms.
We're fighting dogs no enemy likes
And brutally bred to be rid of charm.
We practice on those tied to stakes.
No dog has ever caused more harm.

War dogs supported Spanish Conquests
Across Mexico and the coasts of Peru.
They were bred to be at their fiercest.
Humanity treated like offal residue.
War dogs tracked down native Indians.
Over two thousand were hunted down
And, then, mercilessly mauled to ribbons,
For the greater glory of the Spanish crown.

We've guarded Greek and Roman
Capital, town, citadel, outpost, fort.
Nothing defends better than we can,
Which is why we're so highly sought.
In Corinth, fifty mastiffs forged a garrison.
Yet forty-nine died, having bravely fought.
But Soter escaped and raised the alarm.
Remembered in a marble monument.

In Pizarro's army, dogs fought valiantly,
They were paid regularly like the troops.
No greater fighters, no greater loyalty.
The most committed of all groups,
Whatever the odds or the command.
First to rise and first to attack,
Whether at home or in a foreign land,
Though few ever survived to come back.

Gun Dog Trainer

Gun dogs he loves to train
And with him they wanted to remain.
He values his contracted time.
New dogs are expected to paw the line.

Labradors instinctively understand,
He's a born gun dog training man.
Right from the start,
He can detect dogs who are smart.

He's not a man to cross.
Dogs know he's the boss.
His key qualification -
Training dogs to respond discipline.

He encourages obedience
And to relish every hunting chance.
His greatest and most respected skill
To train a gun dog to retrieve a kill.

Whatever the hour or weather
On wold, moor, dale or highland heather,
His dogs bristle with pride
When they stand at a shooter's side.

He, too, learnt to obey then command
And also come a long, long way
From kennel hand
To winning major gun dog displays.

St. Bernard the Bizarre

No St. Bernard was braver than Ivor,
The supreme mountain rescue climber!
He'd find by his nose
Those lost before they froze -
But, then, half drowned them in saliva!

Woof Wonder Header!

The ball was going wide,
Until a scruffy mongrel bitch
(Though not on either side),
Decided to run across the pitch.

She headed the passing ball
Which flew like a bullet
Smack into the back
Of the Newcastle goal net!

Opposing fans jeered,
While 'Knave of Clubs' fans cheered!
Newcastle players cried, "Foul!"
But the referee allowed the goal.

And, so, the 'Staffs Sunday Cup'
Achieved its unique record -
Fielding the only 'dog player',
Who has ever officially scored!

Why Dogs Have Cold Noses

When the animals trooped into Noah's ark
There was nothing much to do:
Zebras admired their stripes, cows mooed
And elephants lined up in a queue!

Lions were separated from the deer,
Chickens avoided the snake.
Due to their necks, giraffes stayed on deck,
While macaws kept everyone awake!

The dogs were left to do what they liked.
So they strolled about,
And, finally, jumped down into the dark hold
Which they suddenly found.

Down there two dogs were first to spy
A button size hole opening,
Through which flood water steadily flowed,
Causing the Ark to start sinking!

The fast thinking dogs sprang into action -
One dog ran back up to the deck
To seek help, while the other stuck his nose
In the hole to cause a water block.

At first Noah could not understand the reason
For the dog's frantic barking.
His son suggested they should follow the dog
As they'd finished working.

They followed the dog down into the hold,
Until they reached the place
Where the other dog, against the wooden hull,
Was pressing his face!

The flood outside was full of salty brine.
Yet the dog had was bold,
Though whimpering with pain, he remained,
While his nose grew wet and cold.

They lifted the dog away and safely sealed
What was nearly a fatal leak.
They praised the dogs
For the Ark would, surely, have sunk !

The dogs' brave behaviour was observed
By Our Good Lord,
Who decided to keep dogs' noses cold,
As a memory and a reward

Of how two dogs saved Noah's Ark,
In a brave and unique manner.
So, remember, dogs' cold noses to this day
Are tributes of valour!

How to be a Dog Hero

In a small Indian village in South America,
children playing on the edge of the village
disturbed a great wasp nest.

It was a colony of soldier wasps.
The most dangerous wasps in the world.

The colony of soldier wasps erupted
and started to attack the children.

They screamed as only terrified children can
and ran for their lives.
But the children
in their panic,
left a one year old baby behind.

No one tried to save the baby.
It was just too dangerous.

Except the family dog.
He could have been be the first to flee
for he could have run faster than any child.
But what did he do?

He stopped and turned,
when he heard the baby screaming.
and ran back
to the screaming baby
and laid his body over her.

The family dog, the family pet,
took the wasp stings instead of the baby.
Hundreds and hundreds of them.

It was as relentless as being fired at
point blank by a machine gun.
Every bullet, every sting struck home.

Eventually some villagers arrived,
covered by blankets.
and picked up the baby
from under the writhing dog.
The baby survived
due to the protection given by the dog.

The dog died. However, in tribute
to the dog's selfless courage,
the villagers
erected a small statue to the dog.

Is that a dog hero or is that a dog hero ?

World Cup Wagging Winner

In 1966 thieves so corrupt,
Stole the Football World Cup!
Police forces and Interpol
Into action immediately leapt.
But not one policeman did as well
As Pickles, a black and white mongrel.

The one-dog club, out on a training walk
In Norwood, a London suburb,
Spotted something
Wrapped in newspaper under a bush,
And started scratching and scraping.

His owner took a look
And from Pickles the bundle took.
When he opened it up,
He discovered, intact,
The Football World Cup!

Within hours Pickles became
A heroic, international name.
He was paraded before camera crews
For Front Page and TV news.
Pickles took interviews in his stride,
As long as his owner was by his side.
His master also emphasized the case
The World Cup find was to Pickle's taste,
As all balls he loved to chase!

15 Dalmatian Puppies

Asperger's Syndrome froze Thomas's emotion,
Until they adopted Button, a Dalmatian,
Whose pedigree raised expectations
For her father starred in '102 Dalmatians' !

Button proved to be sixteen times better,
Among British records for a Dalmatian litter!
Thomas offered them his undivided attention
And in return, the puppies gave their affection.

Thomas adored the bumper litter of puppies
And volunteered for essential doggy duties -
Fed them, clipped their nails, cleaned their mess
And their relationship blossomed into success.

Fifteen puppies showed Thomas the way,
How to be friendly, joyful and faithful every day.
Thomas began to learn how to give rewards,
To win trust and love with kind and gentle words.

Gone was Thomas's temper tantrums and tears,
The anxious eyes and frequent, frantic fears.
Thomas started to kiss and hug his family,
Which made his parents unbelievably happy.

Along with the puppies, Thomas has grown,
And is now making friends outside his home,
Since fifteen puppies provided the key
To open a child's locked heart and set it free.

Zebra, Zombie and Zonk

The Naming of Dogs seems quite pleasing,
Though some names cause no end of teasing.
Just look at these which have gained renown,
But could drive a dog to a nervous breakdown!

ABC, Abominable, Abracadabra, Africa, Alimony,
Anaconda, Animal, ASAP, ASBO, Asia, Ayatollah.
B-52, Bacon, Bazooka, Beans, Beethoven, Bellyflop,
Bigbelly, Bismarck, Blockhead, Blooper, Blunder,
Bogeyman, Bonkers, Boozer, Brain, Brainchild,
Braindead, Brat, Bubblegum, Bumsteak, Burp, Byte.
Cambridge, Catt, CD-Rom, C.E.O., C.I.A, Choo-
Choo, Clueless,Comma, Cuckoo, Cucumber.
Daffodil, Damage, Database, Desperado, Ding,
Dogmatic, Dong, Dracula, Dunk, Dustmop, Dynamite.
Egghead, Eggnog, Elf, E-Mail, Ennui, Epilogue.
Fingerprint, Flabby, Flirt, Flop, Frankenstein, Freud.
Geewiz, Geezer, Geometrical, Gobbledegook,
Gobbo, Graffiti, Grime, Grumpy, Grunt, Guffaw.
Hermit, Hollywood, Hooligan, Hoodlum, Harpoon.
IBM, Idiocy, Idle, Iguana, Imp, Incorporated, Indent,
Indiscreet, Inexhaustible, Inorganic, Insomnia,
Inspirational, Interpol, Interrogator, IOU, Iscariot, Itch.
Jacuzzi, Jailbait, Jekyll, JFK, Jeopardy, Jughead.
Kafka, Kamikaze, Karamazov, Karloff, Ketchup,
Keyboard, KGB, Killer, Kilo, Kilowatt, Kinky, Kisses,
Knickers, Knockout, Knuckles, Kodiak, Kong, Krakatoa.
Lack, Lager, Laptop, Lasagne, Latrine, Layoff, Lear,
Liability, Lickerish, Looney, Lovechild, Lunatic, Lynch.

Macbeth, Mafia, Michelangelo, Microdot, Microfilm,
Microwave, Misery, Mozart, Mug, Mumbles, Mutant.
Nagger, Nameless, Nappy, Navel, NBA, NBC,
Nebuchadnezzar, Neck, Nectarine, Newspaperman,
Next, Nightmare, Nintendo, Nog, Noisemaker,
Noisette, Noose, Nosferatu, Nostalgia, Nothing,
Odzandends, Ombudsman, Onion, Onomatopoeia,
Opera, Oppenheimer, Orthodox Orville, Oxford.
Panda, Pandemonium, Panfry, Parody, Parsnip,
Pastry, Penguin, Pest, Piano, Pigpen, Pitiful,
Pleasant, Polygamist, Pong, Poof, Porn, Portfolio,
Portly, Printout, Psycho, Pudding, Punk, Puss.
Quadrangle, Quarantine, Quick, Quiet, Quiz, Quoth.
Rage, Razzmatazz, Refrigerator, Rembrandt,
Reptilian, Research, Reverend, RIP, Rugby, Ryot.
Sabotage, Scandal, Scary, Shakespeare, Silly,
Skidder, Skunk, Sloth, Slugger, Sly, Snaggletooth,
Spitball, Splat, Squirt, Stinker, Sweathog, Syrup.
Tablespoon, Tablet, Tabloid, Tacky, Tadpole,
Tagalong, Tamahto, Tantrum, Tasteless, Teacup,
Teapot, Teaspoon, Technicolor, Telex, Telly, Terror,
Throckmorton, Tipsy, Tissue, TLC, TNT, Toad,
Trampoline, Trouble, Tsunami, Turnip, TV, Twerp.
UFO, Uganda, Ultrasonic, Umbrella, Unconscious
Underdog, Untouchable, Uphill, Upkeep, Uproar,
Upshot, Upstart, Uptight, Urchin, Usurper, Utopia.
Vacuum, Vagabond, Vamp, Vandal, Vanish,
Velcro, Velasquez, Vertigo, Vermouth, Vex, Via,
Vicar, Vinaigrette, Viper, Vodka, Voodoo, Vulture.
Wanton, Warmonger, Wart, Watergate, Weeper,
Whatchamacallit, Whatever, Wildcat, Wily, Wilful,
Wilt, Wiseguy, Witch, Wolf Pack, Wrecker, Worm.
X-Man, X-Ray, Xenophon, Xerox, Xmas, Xylophone.

Yelp, Yesterday, YMCA, Yo, Yummy, Yuppie.
'Z', though last is never least,
With three names for canine beasts,
And, surely, decided after too much 'plonk':
Namely - "Zebra, Zombie and Zonk !"

P.S.

Only one in the name list is not true.
A Clue: It describes a way through.

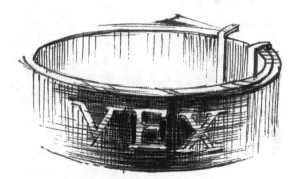

Lover's Leap

When alpha male has left for work,
Downstairs Candy no longer needs to lurk.
He scrambles upstairs,
Hoping to catch his Juliet unawares.

He scurries across the floor
And head butts open the bedroom door.
Full of joy and ardour,
Candy rushes into the boudoir.

He takes a great leap onto the bed
To where his desire is clad.
And there, achieves success
By laying next to his sleeping mistress.

Flying Jet and the Kissing Gates

When Jet was greyhound racing,
He once left the trap and gazed around
As if he wasn't interested in chasing,
For he stood rooted to the ground.
But, then, spotted the pack, off and away,
Which triggered Jet to attack
With another breathtaking display -
Famously and ferociously fast on the track.
Some declared Jet didn't run - he flew!
A flying greyhound without compare,
As Jet surpassed the favoured few
And won the race with space to spare!
But once Jet's racing career was over,
With him would anyone want to bother?

Yet, when Jet retired from racing,
No kinder home could he have wished,
Shared with a whippet called Milly,
Who walked with him by the River Windrush.
Jet received what is offered to so few,
Loving owners who he adores,
Though still wary of half ajar doors.
But when confronted by a kissing gate,
Jet cowered as if recalling the racing trap.
Though Milly was there to demonstrate
It was safe to go through not one, not two,
But three kissing gates along the rabbit walk.
Jet's true nature is now a joy to behold -
The gentlest, friendliest hound in the Cotswold.

Nursing Home Visitors

Residents may spend the day
Looking, thinking, talking,
Reading newspapers,
Completing crosswords,
Watching television,
Doing activities
Or sleeping, dreaming of times past.

But tune into present time,
Alert to the moment,
When Jet and Milly,
A greyhound and whippet,
Enter the lounge.

Residents sit up, lean forward,
Smiles everywhere appear,
As the dogs stand beside them,
Displaying manners fit for a royal court.

Frail hands pat them.
In response, they wag their tails.
Lap up being the focus of attention.
Born ambassadors of the animal kingdom.

And when they depart,
A brighter glow fills the eyes of the resi-
dents,
Who ask,
'When are they coming back?'

Lost in the Glen

Young Jeannie ordered Patch
    Her terrier, to return home again,
For she intended to explore alone
    The mysterious, ten-mile glen.

But loyal Patch still followed her,
    Tho' he knew it wrong,
Until, finally, and most reluctantly,
    Jeannie let Patch tag along.

They ventured into the lonely glen
    Without a bush or tree,
Nor flock, nor herd for company,
    Nor songs from the sea.

Jeannie struggled and climbed,
    Where she never dared before,
Startling deer, grouse, a wild cat,
    And where eagles still soared.

The hours soon slipped away,
    But with food gone and flask dry
Among the marshes on the glen,
    A misty blanket veiled the sky.

Nothing called, nothing moved,
    And the glen soon lost their trust,
For within less than five minutes,
    The glen was engulfed by mist!

Jeannie lurched forward in a daze
    As eerie shadows loomed again,
Making the glen a treacherous maze
    To frighten the bravest of men !

Jeannie could no longer see a path
    And started to stagger and trip !
She nearly fell into the marsh,
    Where it was always fatal to slip !

Tho' all the time by her side,
    Patch didn't falter or swerve !
Jeannie's dog also showed
    How to keep a cheerful nerve !

As Jeannie grew more tired,
    She spoke to Patch one word
To help save her life, "Home!"
    And Patch instantly obeyed !

The terrier led on as if he knew
    The route home by instinct,
While Jeannie followed in despair
    What seemed a futile scent.

For hours Jeannie trailed Patch
    In the direst, darkest glen weather,
Stumbling over rocks and tracks,
    As the mist gathered ever thicker !

But not once did Patch ever halt
    As he led Jeannie - good as blind,
Through the wall of murky mist
    To a home she had failed to find !

Jeannie thought she was lost
    As she followed little Patch
For five weary hours without a rest,
    Until Patch found the croft.

And years later it was regaled
    How Patch saved their Jeannie,
From ever being seen again
    Lost in a mist enshrouded glen !

Nurse and Dog

The Gods can be so unkind,
When Shelli graduated from Nursing School,
She turned blind.
Juvenile diabetes brought the curse
To prevent her becoming a practising nurse.

But courage challenges fate.
Shelli won her unique fight
For a nursing licence from Minnesota state.
She found her vocational call
In the post of Educational Lead Cardiac Nurse.
Holding classes, coaching patients,
Teaching pain management.
Shelli presented life-changing news
To patients with entrenched views,
Who suffered heart attacks, near death misses,
Due to stress, poor life styles, junk food dishes.

Shelli also managed her own life style change
By refusing a white cane or aide support.
Instead she chose Glenda, a black Labrador,
To guide her through every door,
Along hospital wards and department floors.

Whether one patient or a class of hundreds in a hall,
Shellie and Glenda achieved a dream
Working together to demonstrate a team.
Their quiet, unassuming partnership immense.
A nurse with her dog,
Achieving and inspiring independence.

Rusty

His coat was black as a coal pit
And tan blazoned his muzzle and eyes.
Like all Alsatians, Rusty relished action.
He thrived on the hardest tours and trials.

His duty to protect the army regiment
As he patrolled the barracks' borders.
No better reward desired than praise
After obeying his handler's orders.

In the darkest, coldest night
Rusty could detect the scent of any track.
His fearlessness proved again and again
And, on command, would attack.

His handler and father of a young family,
Built an unbreakable bond with Rusty.
When he retired they could not part.
It would have broken their hearts.

And, so, Rusty was given new role -
Not prowlers but two daughters to catch !
If the girls did not come home on time,
Their father would tell Rusty to 'fetch' !

Rusty detected the girls wherever they hid
Behind bush, tree, shed or garden wall.
Gently tugged their skirts to haul them home.
Once more, obeying his master's call.

Death of an Army Dog Handler

Tributes from members
Of the Royal Army Veterinary Corps -
'A man with a passion for his work.
A true professional with an infectious enthusiasm.
Ken always made you smile
And was annoyingly cheerful in the mornings.
He was already someone others looked up to'.
He could have flown home from the frontline.
But he knew his mates were short staffed,
So he decided to stay on.
The next day, as they hunted for booby traps,
Lance Corporal Kenneth Rowe, 24,
And his labrador sniffer dog, Sasha,
Were killed in a Taliban ambush.

K9 Police Dogs

i

K9 - Nicky

Nicky, the German Shepherd, will not alarm
As two hours daily exercise keeps him calm.
He was saved from euthanasia, fortunately,
By the U.S. Coast Guard seeking a trainee.
Now he's a canine drug enforcement officer
And obeys his beloved handler.
'Find! Fetch!" is the key, two-word command
For Nicky to swiftly search for contraband.
Energy and intelligence make him a champ
To confidently search an alligator swamp,
Leap from boats or quietly fly in a helicopter.
No better all-round, four-legged detector!
Yet, away from drugs, Nicky's a playful boy,
Obsessed with a basketball and his toys.

ii

K9 - Major

Dogged detective so aptly applied to Major,
Who, near Cardiff, gave chase to a robber.
The police trained Alsatian kept up the chase,
Even daring to climb a 120-foot quarry face!
Then, through a thick wood, remote and dark,
Major still raced, signalling with a helpful bark.
He then leapt into a freezing river after the thief,
But, there it was felt he'd finally come to grief.
Major answered no call, so the search ended.
Until, four hours later, an Inspector observed
Major, bedraggled, but alert on a door step.
Though the house was searched and checked
Major refused to budge, so they let him enter
And he detected the thief in a wardrobe shelter!

iii

K9 - Zeus

Zeus, an Alsatian, who adores nightly patrols.
Adept, astute, alert, attuned for his work.
So often the first to enter the 'target zone',
Where degrees of evil desperately lurk.
His reputation among the villains assured
For they call Zeus, 'the land shark'!
His pace and power now well-known,
Since appearing on a television programme!
Zeus loves children and his talents and skills
He demonstrates when taken to local schools.
After his efforts Zeus finds no greater delight
Than praise from his police dog handler,
Following another potentially dangerous night,
When, once more, they've kept the streets safer.

iv

K9 - Xena

Xena's supreme sense of smell
Has served Minnesota police very well,
For she'll detect any kind of opiate
To seal a suspected drug dealer's fate.
A Belgian Malinois with a hunting zeal.
A nose from which no drugs are concealed.
She searches suspicious cars as if for fun,
As a highway trooper guards her with a gun.
Xena freezes on finding her 'target',
Before her scratching and barking erupts.
But between dangerous shifts,
Xena stretches forward from her back seat,
To place her head on her owner's shoulder.
A lone female, state trooper driver.

K9 - Lucy

Lucy the Labrador will catch
Most arsonists with a match.
She's become the Great Arson Detective
For her nose is ultra-super sensitive.
Seventeen ignitable liquids she knows
And with each case her expertise grows.
Despite smoke, ashes and fumes
Key clues Lucy soon exhumes.
Among smouldering debris of fire crime,
Lucy gets it right ninety percent of the time.
She'll find minute clues in a suspect's home
And wags her tail as if she's found a bone!
When she identifies the right odour,
A food reward is offered to her.

K9 -Aron

The robber ran from the bank and into the woods
Pursed by Aron the Alsatian and his handler.
They located the suspect who fired two rounds
From two semi-auto handguns.
Without pausing, Aron leapt
In front of the officer to take the fire!
Though fatally wounded,
Aron did not cower, retreat or retire,
But laid over the injured officer
To protect him from another burst of deadly fire.
Aron died in the line of duty,
Displaying a devotion
That exceeded all expectation.
Yet such courage is needed to combat crime,
When serving as a Police Officer - K9.

Ginger

My little Corgi cross
Sends me a card twice a year,
And tho' we're far apart,
He never whimpers or sheds a tear.

My little Corgi cross
Writes to say he's so happy and fine.
Once at Xmas
And then, again, when it's Valentine.

Ginger wins my heart
Whenever I go to see him.
His eyes and coat
Shine brighter than a sunbeam.

He's been re-homed three times
But its always broken down.
It seems to me my little Corgi cross
Prefers the Dogs Trust.

He's their longest resident
And given toys, balls and bones;
And adores his favourite walk,
Up to their garden of little headstones.

~~~~~~~

Ginger (1995 -2008) - sponsored dog at the Dogs Trust
Re-homing Centre, Evesham, England.

Ode to Dogs

Once of the wolf and the wilderness
But, now, patted, petted and kissed.
No greater or more devoted loyalist.
A protector when an owner is at rest.
He only asks to be fed, walked, loved
To win bright eyes and a wagging tail.
Surely, a guardian from heaven above.
Faithful follower before breeze or gale.
Every dog deserves more than a bone -
A delight and joy, a tonic for our health,
As a family pet or for those living alone.
His affection greater than any wealth.
Entirely trusts his handler with his fate.
His life, his spirit, his love immense.
His only fear if they should separate.
Yet, even then, would use every sense
To scour the trail, no matter the miles,
To see again his owner's loving eyes.
He asks no questions and tells no lies.
A dog will stand by whatever the trials:
When your riches and titles are gone,
And family and friends become few,
Your dog stays constant as the sun,
And remains true whatever you do.
A dog will bravely risk limb and life,
Whether mongrel or highborn hound,
If their owners confront danger or strife,
They admirably serve wherever found,
Bringing an honest beauty into our lives.
And, finally, when they no longer bound,
In our hearts their fond memory survives.

'Rats', a dog soldier

When times are dark
Heroes tend to make their mark.
So, praised in many a log,
The heroism of a corgie cross dog.

His name was Rats.
Once high among snipers' targets,
For it never took long
For Rats to detect a hidden bomb.

Happy in his pack,
Billeted in the regiment's barrack.
Loyal to his men
From Belfast to Crossmaglen.

An army professional,
Who always answered the call,
Whether day or night,
Patrolling streets or on a chopper flight.

He would lead out ahead.
Yet, in a second, could be dead.
A firebomb didn't fail.
It burnt four inches off his tail.

Yet Rats remained fine,
Despite metal trapped in his spine,
And shotgun pellets
Embedded across his little chest.

During dangerous times
Rats remained in the front line,
Twice run over by cars,
That permanently bent his front paws.

But worse than any bullets
Was changing masters with new units.
So often it broke his heart,
When a beloved master had to depart.

Rats was without peer
As a four footed, serving soldier.
His devotion to duty
Made him a national celebrity.

He was sent many treats,
From jumpers to doggie sweets,
And two sacks of letters a day,
Took six soldiers to answer.

But, above all,
He raised every soldier's morale.
"An oasis in a desert
Of sadness," described a conscript.

Rats led countless patrols
On searches and defensive roles.
Walking briskly ahead,
Never believing he could soon be dead.

His rising injuries
Suffered on perilous active duties,
Never caused to fail
The little mongrel from wagging his tail.

But the vet's decision was made
And Rats led a famous passing-out parade;
Two medals awarded
And in regimental dispatches recorded.

Then, retired to Kent,
To track down grouse and pheasant,
And live a happier life
Far from war, danger and strife.

The King's Spaniel and the Poet

Once the favoured pet of His Majesty,
Unique at Court, the Royal Spaniel.
Surely, assured of a pampered destiny,
Until cast off for being too old and ill.
The aristocracy scorned his infirmity,
But it roused a poet's wrath and pity,
As the spurned pet begged in the city.
Deep compassion births generosity -
Agrippa rescued the stricken spaniel,
Whose plight he penned into poetry.
So, evermore, the world knew well,
The King proved pitiless and petty;
And nothing could be much worse,
When the crown is cursed by verse.

The poet Agrippa d'Aubigny (1552 - 1603) rescued the
royal spaniel abandoned by the French King Henri V1,
for being too old.

Three in a Bed

Her new neighbour started to turn bright red
When Eve declared, 'We sleep three in a bed!'
Meaning Joe, her husband,
And Milly, her Dachshund,
Who snuggled up to Eve as if they were wed!

Tell-Tale Trail

Dean adored his little pet
Jake, a Jack Russell,
Which was easy to tell as Dean
Took him to work as well.

Dean did a job
Which was very particular,
Working nights;
The best time for a burglar.

Dean broke into a house
When it was very late,
And to the stair post
He tied Jake, his best mate.

But Dean was soon disturbed,
And decided to flee,
Rather than risk being caught
And losing his liberty.

Though Dean forgot,
And to the post Jake remained tied.
So, when the police arrived,
At the dog they stared in surprise!

They let Jake loose and followed him
Along the tell tale trail,
Which led police to Dean's home,
Exchanged for 15 months in jail!

Chance

A bull terrier on London's streets
In 1882 had nowhere to go.
Hardly given a second chance,
Yet would soon become a hero.

When the fire brigade arrived
In Fleet Street they saw
The bull terrier amid the smoke,
Frantically barking at a locked door.

When the firemen broke it down
Round them black smoke swirled,
And the desperate cries from within
Of a trapped, terrified young girl.

When they rescued the girl,
The dog barked and jumped with elation,
And followed the fire brigade
Back to Chandos Street Fire Station.

The dog would not leave the station
And so, was adopted by the brigade,
Sleeping with their horses in the stable
And always keen to be a helping aid.

They soon named him, 'Chance',
Due to the way he had arrived - 'by Chance'!
And he wore his collar with such pride,
As a full time member of the fire brigade.

The collar also contained the inscription:
"Stop me not but onward let me jog.
For I am Chance,
The London firemen's dog."

Chance proved his worth as a fire-fighter,
Racing through smoke faster than the firemen.
He soon sniffed out the injured,
And through the thickest smoke quickly ran.

He even created his own way
Of accessing a burning building,
By pressing hard his bottom against glass
And entering backwards while barking!

Chance saved so many from fire
And also held up a little boy by his coat,
To stop him from drowning in the Thames,
Until rescue arrived by river boat.

But Chance was doomed by fate
When he went out on one fire call.
He was fatally wounded
From a collapsing house wall.

They took Chance back to the station,
Where the fire bell started to ring
Still Chance tried to go,
But the effort proved too much for him.

Chance staggered and died in the arms
Of Dick Tozer, one of the firemen.
A dog who exceeded every expectation
And received the highest commendation
In his plated inscription:

'Chance'

The Dog Hero of Chandos Street Fire Station.

Labrador Wild Boar Hero

The most terrifying fight you've ever seen
Took place in the Forest of Dean,
Between two wild boars
And Harvey, Kate's pet Labrador.

Kate had stepped along the path
That led to a litter of piglets!
Against a lone woman
Charged the wild boar parents!

Kate felt her heart fill with terror
Before two rampaging wild boars!
But Harvey stood full square in front of her
And gave a growl like a lion's roar!

Regardless of the risks,
Harvey took on their razor sharp tusks.
A dog like no other,
He charged, and bowled them both over!

Barks and snorts, growls and screams,
Rang out across the Forest of Dean!
But it was the wild pigs who backed down
And heroic Harvey who wore the victor's crown !

Afghan Hound

Her eyes glisten black as coal
    And peer right into your soul.
Yet seem from heaven above,
    For how they gleam with love!

A well-bred, noble hound
    Who hardly makes a sound;
And a flowing coat in flight
    When his prey is in sight!

Few could chase any faster,
    When ordered by her master.
She's a hunter natural-born,
    And rules the fields of Sherborne.

They wait behind hedges low
    Until the rabbits begin to show.
Then her master lets her slip
    To bring a buck back in her grip.

Streamlined to meet her needs,
    The Afghan Princess of Speed!
Yet welcomes his gentle hands,
    Whose love she understands.

Like some love-struck fan
    She adores her young man.
The commander of her days,
    She gladly follows and obeys.

Beauty of the Blitz

They declared dogs could never be used
In the Blitz to find those buried alive,
Because contrasting fumes would confuse a dog
No matter how hard he might strive.
But no-one told Beauty, management's views,
Who dutifully kept her master company
As his animal rescue squad scoured a fiery hell.
Then one night, Beauty was let free,
And instantly applied her supreme sense of smell,
Which detected something beneath
The smouldering debris of a bombed out house.
Beauty began to bark and scratch,
Causing the rescue workers to shift their focus
And to find, under festering ruins, a cat.
Yet they had also discovered what would be
Deemed in rescue work an historic moment,
Having found the first 'Sniffer Dog,' Beauty.

In Memory of Bari

A Nazi officer shot Bari, the St. Bernard, dead.
Who allegedly, tried to attack a search squad.
When little Jan heard of the murder of his pet,
For the next seven decades his heart grieved.

Companions since Jan was just four years old,
Bari was the gentlest, kindest dog in creation.
His murder on the streets of Kracow epitomized
The injustice and inhumanity of the Nazi invasion.

Jan spent days grieving for the loss of his pet,
And vowed he would make the murderers pay.
He enlisted as a teenager in the Resistance
That was dedicated to driving the Nazis away.

But, one day, Jan was arrested and imprisoned
Under suspicion, before a Gestapo interrogation.
Three Nazis tried to make Jan confess his role,
That would have guaranteed public execution.

Jan refused to admit he joined the Resistance,
As he watched the German Alsatian on the floor.
Half the size of Barie, yet a fierce beast to others,
But he stirred in Jan memories of Bari even more.

Jan thought of Bari, his beloved companion,
At the moment he should have shook with fear.
When they threatened to let the Alsatian loose,
But Jan stayed calm for he felt Bari was near.

Unable to break his nerve the interrogation ended.
Jan survived and knew what made him brave.
His memories of Bari gave him a deeper strength
And saved him from a martyred teenager's grave.

Grenade Carrier

One Great War photo never fades
Of a German messenger dog's role -
Carrying a bag of hand grenades
To soldiers under fire in a shell hole.

The dog makes a poignant attempt
As the soldier unstraps the delivery,
To rub his head against his chest.
Seeking comfort prior to their expiry.

Never Lick Strangers

Snowy the poodle was a friendly chap,
He'd eagerly leap on a stranger's lap!
Which wasn't wise
And, so, no surprise,
When he became victim of a dognap!

Delta

24 August, 79 *AD

When Mount Vesuvius finally erupted
Of one dog it could be expected,
That Delta would remain in Pompeii,
Despite night smothering day.
He did not cower or hide, flinch or flee.
He loyally stood by his revered family.
His collar revealed Delta's devotion
To his master, Severinus, and his little son.

Such adoration affirmed in a tragic way,
When over the boy, Delta bravely lay,
As toxic fumes and ash shrouded the city.
Delta stayed and fulfilled his doomed duty.
He could easily have escaped death,
But with a child chose to share his last breath.
No greater call or higher expectation
Could match such a selfless, gallant action.

His brave behaviour accorded him
A revered place in canine history.
On his collar, once glistening with pride,
Other deeds of heroism also inscribed:
How he saved his master, Severinus,
From turbulent waves high and dangerous.
Drove off four thieves about to harm
His trapped master who raised the alarm.

He rescued Severinus, once more,
From a ravenous she-wolf waging war.
And what further proof does one need
Than Delta's four heroic, fearless deeds,
To demonstrate that man's best friend
Will defend his beloved to the bitter end?
Like a solitary star loyal to the great sun,
Delta protected his master and small son.

My Old Dog

He's now fifteen years old
And not as lively as he used to be,
But keeps me warm when I'm cold
By snuggling close up to me.

He does not leap as before
To greet me when I open the door,
But knows I understand
When he licks my outstretched hand.

He no longer runs along the lane
As far as my eyes can see.
Though his love will never wane
For he only wants to be near me.

He rarely growls or barks
And his arthritis slows up our walks.
Yet I don't need to wonder why,
He so often likes to sleep and sigh.

He tends to halt before a ball.
But will slowly wag his tail,
When I hold the lead and call
To walk along our shortened trail.

He slowly prowls around,
Sniffing some scent he's found.
Yet, whatever the time or place,
He retains his dignity and grace.

He no longer climbs the stairs
But likes to rest beside my chair.
He no longer buries his bone
Or wants to wander and roam.

Though better days we've known,
Together we've never felt alone.
Yet his time will shortly come,
Like the going down of the sun.

Now he rarely plays,
But before the fire lays,
And my slippered foot will allow
To stroke his tummy soft and slow.

I'm also very old
And feel the coming of the cold.
My only wish when all is done,
My old dog will be the first to pass on.

Borzoi Bookshop Dog Duo

When I open the bookshop door,
Bubbly comes trotting across the floor.
An eleven-year-old Jack Russell,
Who loves a friendly 'fussell'!

I seem to have passed some test,
And feel like a special guest,
As Bubbly rolls over on the floor,
Keen to be tickled for evermore!

But she's not alone,
Tyke the Staffie appears with a bone.
Not to be outdone,
He also wants to join in the fun!

Tyke's tip-top favourite treat,
He drops right next to my feet!
I throw the bone a little way
And Tyke fetches it back straight away!

Buddies, pals, mates, chums together
Who never cause any bother!
Closer than canine twin brothers,
They even sleep alongside each other.

They're such a wonderful, winsome two,
I forget what I've come in to do!
In fact, they're such a hit,
If I wrote a book I'd put them both in it!

Monty and the Crown Jewels

In the 1920s Little Monty
Was King of The Mongrels,
For he helped to guard
The British monarch's Crown Jewels.

Until the Tower of London
Installed a new state of the art alarm
To prevent thieves
Causing the crown jewels any harm.

Monty, it would seem,
Who had given visitors such delight,
Would soon be
Virtually unemployed overnight.

But when he ran under the detector levels,
Monty suddenly revealed
A fatal fault which thieves could explore,
For it had not been sealed!

Best of all,
Assembled among notable witnesses,
Nothing less
Than the world's now laughing press!

Yet, when the news broke,
Monty was deemed a hero evermore,
Defending the crown jewels
By exposing the new alarm's fatal flaw!

Puppies

Which one can I choose ?
He's so cute, and so is he!
How adorable they are!
What creatures are more lovely?

How playful, soft and warm
And they want to be cuddled by me.
They're so divine. Did heaven
Send them by special delivery ?

Only one? Can't I have two?
I love him and him - or is it a her?
Oh, look at those brown eyes!
There's no heart they couldn't stir.

Look, look! He's licking my hand!
Oh, I just don't know who to pick!
Please, please, PLEASE,
Can we adopt all six?

'Citizen Kane 9'

To compete with multiplexes direct,
A cinema attracted owners and their pets.

Pet dogs in the Admiral Cinema, Vienna,
Soon proved enormously popular.

Dogs admitted free every afternoon
And given a blanket, water and popcorn.

The sound system is turned down a bit,
So dogs' ears will not be hurt.

In fact, what can possibly beat
Lying half-asleep beside your owner
On a cinema seat?

Where it's warm, cosy and half-dark,
And joining in celluloid music or talk.

With a whimper, woof or bark,
Some dogs even prefer it to a walk!

Indeed, owners all agree,
Their dogs adore a good movie,
Which really is no surprise -

For the Film Voted Best of All Time
Usually is 'Citizen Kane 9' !

Emma

1986 - 2007

A popular supermarket worker
And devoted dog lover.
Never sought publicity,
Accustomed to anonymity.

Until she was in a car
That hit a dog in the rush hour.
Emma told the driver to stop
And ran back to the stricken pet.

Her aim, to save the dog
From another four wheeled attack.
But, then, she herself
By a car was fatally struck!

Emma's dog rescue mission,
Driven by selfless compassion.
At twenty one,
Her life over and done.

The Dog Stonings

Take the case - totally true -
Of the dog who married a Hindu.
Seva Kuman, 33, married mongrel Selvie
To alter his 'ill-starred destiny',
And help erase the curse
That had made his life worse and worse.

Fifteen years before, Seva committed a crime
That further festers with the passing of time.
His rage mercy could not assuage.
Seva's wrath sought and wrought death,
When he committed the terrible sin
Of stoning two dogs to death.

We know not why, only that two dogs died.
But evil cannot hide.
Imagine stone after stone
Breaking bone after bone.
Even their last whimper,
Could not douse Seva's red hot temper.

But murder, if anything,
Not a whiff of happiness will ever bring.
As for two murdered, what can we say,
They shall surely stalk, both night and day.
Indeed those two dogs did not die in vain,
A greater force avenged their pain.

Seva, the farm worker, soon after found
He could no longer work the ground.
His legs and hands became paralyzed
As if, in the Stars, he was now despised.
His livelihood sentenced to death.
He also found he had gone deaf.

In fact, Life had become so bad,
Seva believed he would next go mad.
Despised by his neighbours,
Seva, in despair, consulted an astrologer,
Who advised marriage to a canine
To lift the Curse of his Dog Stoning Crime.

And so, Seva wedded Selvi, the mongrel,
Hoping she'd guide him out of his living hell,
But whether it went well, only time will tell.
The moral being never kill a dog,
For you may unleash an Avenging God,
Who will not spare the Wrath of His Rod.

Doga

In keep-fit, keep-well California,
Dogs attend classes in Yoga.
Their innate charm
Keeps owners calm.
So, Yoga, there, is declared Doga!

Barge Sabotage

For retired Reg and Lil
Barge-boat life on the canal
Proved far too tranquil.

So they adopted Cliff,
A German Shepherd,
Who soon became bored stiff.

Too help time pass,
Cliff chewed through
The barge underside fibreglass.

Before they could wink,
Or begin to think,
The barge started to sink!

But Cliff's action reaped a reward.
For a few frantic minutes,
No longer was anyone bored!

'Angels from Heaven'

Josh was a ten-year-old boy
with Down's Syndrome.

He got lost in the woods of Montana
For three 'bone chilling days'
Before he was rescued.
Josh had mild frostbite on all ten toes.
Otherwise, he was in good health.

When taken to the ambulance
Two stray dogs tried to accompany him,
A dachshund and a heeler.

It was maintained that Josh
Could not have survived without support.
Therefore, it was suggested
The two stray dogs had displayed
The following life saving actions -

With temperatures below zero at night,
The dogs kept Josh warm
By cuddling close to him.

As Josh was not dehydrated
It was thought that the dogs
Led him to water.

The dogs also provided companionship,
So Josh did not feel abandoned.

Following the rescue,
Questions were raised -

Were the dogs lonely ?
Did they need company ?
Was their behaviour a form of submission
Or obedience to a prospective master?

Josh was a complete stranger
And the dogs had no reason
To help a child with a severe disability,
And to keep him warm, watered and hopeful.

Although, some dog specialists described
The dogs actions as
'An example of the sense of compassion.'
The dogs felt an instinctive need
To protect a vulnerable child.

Josh's mother said,
'The dogs fell in love with my son
During those days.'
She also described the dogs as
'Angels from Heaven.'

Josh's family adopted both dogs,
Who saved the life of their son.

Napoleon and the Dog on the Battlefield

Napoleon Bonaparte struggled to abide
With the pleas of a dead soldier's dog,
Howling with grief at his master's side.
Both victims of a great battle in Italy.
It sullied the conquest for Napoleon
For what was another, stunning victory,
When the distressed dog ran up to him,
Desperately imploring the Emperor's aid.
His personal 'Emperor' had fatally fallen.
Death claimed the ultimate commission.
The dog as bereft as a star without its sun.
Napoleon declared no deeper impression
Upon him could he have ever believed,
Than that grieving dog on the battlefield.

Brandy

He did not know what it meant
To join the Royal Marines Regiment;
Trained and disciplined to be
Committed to his destiny in the Army.

A new life, with no turning back,
Once assigned to Special Duties in Iraq.
The hours active and long,
And not one paw does he put wrong.

He leads where few would go,
Accompanied by his dog handler commando.
He obeys every command
To sniff out explosives hidden in the sand.

He doesn't flinch at all,
Though bullets may fly from behind a wall.
And barks right on time,
When he discovers a booby trap mine.

Brandy, the black Labrador,
The whole unit has come to adore.
He's their unofficial mascot,
Who adores every soldier's hug and pat

One Bark Wonder

At birth both Collies so cute.
Yet Mickey remained mute
Who stayed silent but faster
Than Bob, who left their master,
When selected and taken away
To learn hill shepherding every day.

Mickey stayed in the dale
And rarely did he ever falter or fail
Against thorns, brambles, thistles.
He obeyed all commands and whistles.
But never did anyone hear
Of him barking in all his career.

He was good and calm,
And so his silence caused alarm.
Mickey was a clever boy,
But never expressed warning or joy.
A silent dog raises concerns,
When everything else he quickly learns.

Then, at the Sheepdog Trials
Which Bob clearly won by miles,
Just as they put the rosette
On Bob's gleaming, pounding chest,
Mickey gave his leash a jerk
Before making his first, and last, bark!

His family gasped with surprise,
For they quickly surmised
Mickey recognised Bob, his brother,
From puppy times together,
And at the moment of Bob's award
Mickey gave a 'Brotherly Bark Reward' !

Barping Not Barking

In the car Monty was told to remain,
But eventually decided to complain -
By pressing the horn
To express his pain
Left alone by his owners' - yet again !

Just Our Joey

This is about Joey our dog,
Who I think is really great.
Dad got him for a Xmas gift
From the pet stall in the market.

He's our very own black Labrador,
Who we all love and adore.
His eyes are coal black
And my little sister rides on his back.

Joey's a dog we all trust
And loves a buttered crust.
We take him for walks again and again,
And play ball with him in our garden.

He often tries to give me a sticky lick,
Which I wipe away really quick.
But I'm the only one who can bear
Picking up pieces of his hair.

Our Dad he simply adores
And follows him through all the doors.
I watch Joey when he yawns at night.
His teeth are huge and can really bite.

He'll try to sleep on the sofa
As well as in the back of the car.
But, sometimes, he goes to sleep
When he lays his head on my little feet.

The Big, Fat, Long Sausage Dog

I much prefer the sound
Of being called, "A Dachshund"!
But, I'm afraid to say,
My weight is so great
It's made me long, fat and round,
And my belly now scrapes the ground!

Though my belly doesn't just sag,
I must confess it actually drags!
To the embarrassing extent,
When I waddle along the pavement,
I get so bruised and sore,
I don't want to go for walks anymore!

But how did this come about
That I've become so very stout ?
It's my owner's fault ! In fact, she's also fat
And would have much preferred a cat!
She stuffs herself and me with far too much food,
Which I eat because I feel I should!

So, here I am, looking far older than my age,
Panting along like a great, fat, long sausage!
I can hardly bark or growl
But, because of my weight, I want to howl,
Which makes it even worse.
Being big, fat, long sausage dog is a curse!

There's only one thing left I can do,
Limit how much I want to chew.
I'll also shed further pounds
If I chase balls in parks and grounds,
And no longer sleep in front of the telly,
As I strive to shorten my great, long, fat belly!

Hello, what's that? Half a pork pie.
Are you trying to make me cry ?
Well actually its just a little treat,
And surely won't take long to eat!
It smells so good full of pork,
And I can eat it without a knife or fork!

There we are, it's all gone.
And of course, it didn't take very long!
Now, what was I saying before I ate?
Oh yes, I suppose I should get
A little thinner here and there,
And then people might not so often stare!

So, it's a strict diet I'll start.
It'll help my belly and my heart.
I intend to play a new keep fit role
And only eat half of what's in my bowl.
Hello. what's that ? A cheese crisp!
Well, surely, just one won't prove a fatal risk!

Oh, yes, it does! My size has got worse!
I'm now so big I feel I'm about to burst!
My owner looks so upset,
Before she rings the vet!
I feel a rumbling in my belly
As its churning like a bowl of jelly!

Oh dear, oh lor, oh lummy!
I don't like the sound of my tummy!
Oh no! I've blown up like a balloon!
Now I'm floating around the room,
And suddenly explode in a hundred ways
Scattering curry, crisps and bolognese!

Oh, no! Its not a laugh !
I've found I've just burst in half!
My head and body are on the telly
While my tail and lower bit
On the sofa now tries to sit !
I reckon I'm right back off to the vet !

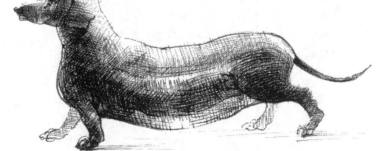

Mr Nyme's Pets

Mr Nyme finally achieved dubious glory
In a five-paragraph tabloid story,
Doomed in his freezing bed-sitting room.
A high side wall ensured daily gloom.

When his body was four days old
They found him. Killed by the cold.
Beside him at the bitter end,
His two pets. His only family and friends.

Sammy, his nine-year-old mongrel.
Half terrier, half spaniel.
Molly, his old ginger cat, also stayed,
Looking out of the window most of the day.

When they broke in, Mr Nyme was grey.
Sammy still barked to keep them away.
Loyal to the last. Nor did Molly go quietly.
She hissed from behind the old settee.

Their owner's past, a closed mystery.
Just a dog and cat, his surviving family.
The three of them battling everything.
And Mr Nyme, their recognised king.

Street Dog Survivors

Its not all sad, mad and bad,
Curled up on the pavement
Beside their homeless owner.
At least someone wants them.
In fact, they comfort each other.
Two against a stone-faced world.

Vets have said such dogs are eligible
For free check-ups, vaccinations.
Indeed, in his televised opinion,
Street dogs were among
The fittest dogs he'd ever seen.
Pavement pooches aren't slouches.

Street dogs, it seems,
Thrive on streets, river banks, parks.
Interiors weaken them:
Central heating, toys, knitted coats.
Simply sullies their spirit
Like rust corrodes metal.

In the concrete jungle,
Lessons are quickly learned.
Enduring all weathers.
Sharpening up in body and mind.
Getting ever leaner, fitter, harder.
Dog survivor inside, emerges or dies.

'Cat' Dog of the Year

Dogs befriending cats can never really work,
Unless you live in Long Beach, New York.
Where cats seek out the company
Of Ginny, an amazing Schnauzer-Husky.

On Ginny's walks stray cats appear
And for this dog none of them show fear!
Ginny's become a Saviour of the Homeless
As the cats are long past their best -
Unloved, thin, distressed, deaf, even kittens.
Survive on scraps from gutters and bins.

The irony it should be a canine
Who leads them to a new home again.
Cats who choose to come near
Are placed in the Mobile Cat Carrier.
And, then, once examined by the vet,
Usually transferred to a Cat Shelter direct.

So far, 546 rescues passed,
And you can be sure they're not the last.
Westchester Feline Club even named
Ginny 'Cat of the Year' for rescues claimed.

I Wanted a Dog

I wanted a dog to lie on the mat,
    But we went and adopted a cat.

I wanted a dog to welcome me home,
    But our cat likes being left alone.

I wanted a dog to be my best chum,
    But our cat only likes Mum.

I wanted to see a dog's adoring eyes,
    But our cat just gives haughty smiles.

I wanted to dog to chase a ball in the park,
    But our cat would think that odd work.

I wanted a dog who'll obey me,
    But our cat behaves independently.

I wanted to hear a dog's bark and woof,
    But our cat chooses to stay aloof.

I wanted a dog to sleep on my bed,
    But our cat prefers the sofa instead.

I wanted a dog I could love and tickle,
    But our cat remains cool and fickle.

I've a wanted a dog all my life,
    Alas, our cat is adored by my wife.

Plato Not Pluto

When Plato won 'The Talking Dog Award',
Cambridge proudly applauded.
Until they heard
What Plato said,
"By the way, I was actually born in Oxford."

Daisy in the Window

If to Stratford-upon-Avon you should go,
A most delightful attraction
Adorns a lady's clothes shop front window.
Below the most elegant of clothes
Daisy, a Yorkshire terrier,
Against the window presses her little nose!

Strangers passing smile and sometimes stop,
When Daisy catches their eye.
Some declare she's the mascot of the shop.
Daisy wears a perfectly tailored, permanent coat,
As you would expect
When the address is a fashion shop of note.

She loves to watch folk strolling past,
And when they come near
Wags her tail like a little black and brown mast.
Daisy adores customers who enter and stay,
Brings them her toys
To lay at their feet, hoping they'll agree to play !

She often pirouettes over the polished floor,
And 'talks' to customers
With a chatty yap while offering a friendly paw.
Daisy's appearance and actions
Have, of course, turned her
Into One of Stratford's Superior Canine Icons!

Fear of Walkies

Sam's owner was old and frail
And could not let Sam out on the trail.

For twelve years she kept her beloved pet
Inside her reclusive and exclusive apartment.

Sam fulfilled every expectation
As a cross German alsatian -

He obeyed orders to remain inside the flat,
Where he grew up, ate, slept, played and sat.

The Great Outdoors he never went near,
Even the window view filled him with fear.

Sam was a dog in a million, of course,
Who grew up to bark and balk at walks !

When his owner passed on Sam was placed
In a dog's home - but Outdoors still could not face !

He'd howl and dig his claws in the ground,
The first dog agoraphobic they'd found.

But as Sam simply refused to roam,
They decided to keep him in at the home.

And gave Sam the thickest quilt they could afford
With lots of toys so he wouldn't get bored !

The Listener

How can victims divulge their grief
And restore their self-belief ?
Who can help them explain
And so ease the pressure of their pain ?

Among the depressed, could an animal
Interact better than a 'professional' ?
A chaplain's dog passes that test
Of how to support people in crisis.

Scruffy stays by their side,
Comforts those whose loved one has died.
Nuzzles them when they cry.
Her well of patience never runs dry.

Scruffy senses deeper emotions
And soon nurtures trusted relations.
She listens with glowing eyes,
Confidantes consider loving and wise.

Scruffy's told things by the bereaved
That makes them so often feel relieved.
A trained therapist dog who may not know
She brings the sun wherever she goes.

A dog with outstanding recovery rates -
Third Top Therapist Dog in the United States.

Double Cheers !

Algy the Labrador adored his bowl of beer.
But, afterwards, if anyone sat too near,
They soon found
After one round,
He'd burp together from both front and rear!

Party Animals

Toby, an adorable Jack Russell,
Was given a sumptuous 'do',
And his dearest friends invited too
Mr Mole, the growling Mongrel,
And Bouncer, the Alsatian,
Whose 'party piece' was to howl !

The cost of the party was high -
Five thousand pounds made many sigh !
At a Bournemouth club, the deputy mayor
And a hundred and fifty two-legged guests,
Celebrated the memorable 'feast'!

The dog-inspired menu
Caused a salivating canine queue,
As noted by a society reporter:
Slurped egg and milk cocktail shake,
scoffed prime beef and liver,
and wolfed kennel shaped birthday cake.

Although Toby was unaware the fine fare
And the presence of the deputy mayor,
Was for tender services he rendered,
When his owner felt his life had ended.
Toby's grateful owner declared
His dog's lavish party was the chance
To reward Toby's affection, that saved his life
When suicidal after a broken romance.

The Bull Terrier of Batsford Lane

Rollo waddles along Batsford Lane,
A four-legged companion in the rain.
He's 'christened' most of the trees
And looks as pleased as can be!

A bustling, buoyant, black bull terrier,
Who clutches a branch in rainy weather.
Rollo grips his take-home prize,
As they descend from the rain swept rise.

How he swaggers along the lane,
Unaware of how he also entertains -
For that big, black branch
Feels as good as a bone for lunch!

His black coat and white necked vest
Makes him look like a posh dinner guest!
And when he woofs and barks,
He's clearly making sensible remarks!

Yet, Rollo's unaware of how he brings
Such joy from the smallest things.
His black eyes glowing so bright,
Make a walk in the rain like a stroll in sunlight!

Whatever needs to be done,
Rollo always behaves like its a bit of fun!
He's such a friendly, joyful chappie
He makes everyone feel really happy!

Dog Questionnaire

The question most dogs tend to send -
Do you want me be my friend ?
What other animal so easily attracts,
Or causes strangers to stop in their tracks ?
Who displays such intense devotion
And senses your deepest emotion ?
Who shows the brightest of eyes,
Where absolute and lasting love lies ?
What do titles and riches really mean,
When only you are wanted to be seen ?
Who would believe a dog's greatest fear,
Is when their owner is no longer near ?
So, what better can an owner offer in return,
Than a loving home and to be kind but firm ?

The Loyalty of Hachiko

Two-year-old Hachiko was full of expectation
As he waited at Shibuya railway station,
For his master, a professor at Tokyo University,
To whom he displayed Akita breed loyalty.

Hachiko met the train every afternoon,
And ran to his master as soon as he saw him.
But one bitterly cold day in 1925,
Hachiko waited in vain for his master to arrive.

No more trains would his master ride,
For at the University the professor had died.
His friends found a new home for Hachiko,
But every day to the rail station he'd go.

Though his master never came,
At the station Hachiko faithfully remained.
This happened every day for ten years,
And moved plenty of passengers to tears.

Old friends tried to tempt Hachiko away,
But to the train station he went every day.
In the evening he always appeared there,
Awaiting his owner to come back as before.

No where else did Hachiko want to go
And, so, was given food by local vendors.
The new station master also took pity on him
And set aside a place for him in the storeroom.

Not one day did Hachiko ever miss,
Despite getting old with creeping arthritis.
Strangers came to feed and pat him,
Which also brought satisfaction to them.

Passengers raised a fund to collect
For a statute of Hachiko to erect,
Displayed at Shibuya Railway Station
In recognition of his outstanding devotion.

When twelve, Hachiko died on the spot
Where his master always greeted him.
A Day of National Mourning was duly held
And a Monument to Hachiko declared.

So, the dog who proved loyal to one man,
Became a National Treasure of Japan;
And for children no better example to show,
The spirit of family loyalty than that by Hachiko.

The Twelve Million Dollar Dog

Have you ever heard of a dog so filthy rich
As 'Trouble', a New York pampered pooch,
When her owner passed on,
'Trouble' inherited twelve million -
While two grandchildren were left not a stitch!

Yet, even for dogs,
Too much wealth DAMAGES Health.
In fact, being rich is a bitch.
What's the point of being a multimillion mutt,
If you can't sniff another pooch's butt?
Trouble's inheritance also gave the chance
To be hounded by death and kidnap threats!

No longer could Trouble dare go for a walk
In her beloved City of New York!

They thought Trouble would be safer by far
In a remote hideaway in Florida.
A flight hijack they tried to fumble
By naming her 'Bauble' instead of Trouble!

And, so somewhere in the Sunshine State,
A Maltese terrier lives out her legendary fate.
Though she can't linger long to sniff or pee
Because she's the richest dog in history,
With a potential ransom
Dognappers will always find
Mouth-wateringly, droolingly handsome!

Sam the Surfer

No four-legged surfer is keener
Than Sam the terrier of Argentina.

He's become internationally known
As the little mutt whose mastered foam.

Sam's the star of the surfers' show,
Where other pets fear to go!

Yet he's kept secure all the time,
Due to a safety line.

Tied to his wooden board,
As he eagerly looks for a wave to hoard.

When he's skimming over the rolling sea,
His little tail can be seen wagging merrily!

Sam's having such terrific fun,
Standing on South American surf in the sun!

There's nothing he likes better than a ride
On the incoming, crashing tide!

And his joy soon spreads to everyone,
When he's shown worldwide on television!

Black Dog Outdogged

Deep depression dominated
after a difficult death in Nancy's family.
She just wanted to stay at home.
Outdoors terrified her.

Glen, her black and tan mongrel,
sensed her fear. But whined for his walks.

Somehow she forced herself
to take Glen out. She remembered
her legs shaking as she opened
the front door.

It was like standing before an abyss.

Nancy's heart thumped like a piston.
Her first steps on the pavement
felt like stepping into Death Valley.

But Glen looked up at her,
urging her to keep moving.

He gently tugged on the lead,
as if to say, "Its alright. You're not alone.
I'm here to help you. You're safe with me.
Come on, we can do this."

After a week of daily walking the dog,
she felt her confidence slowly returning,
and told her friends it was due to
the daily taking of Glen's 'natural medicine'.

But it was rejected by medical officials,
that the dark and mighty forces
of depression and agoraphobia,
could possibly be cured by
'a run of the mill, little mongrel'.

However, dog lovers would conclude
it was a clear case of 'black dog'
being outdogged by a quite exceptional
'run of the mill, little mongrel.'

'Black dog' - an old metaphor to describe depression

Dog Mansion

Miss Felicity Pyne lived in a Surrey mansion,
Where she indulged her lifelong passion -
Raising dogs who she believed so nice,
They truly deserved their own paradise.

Her adored parents had passed away,
So she was in charge night and day.
In the mansion's elegant, cultivated grounds
A dog paradise Miss Pyne decided to found.

Whenever she met a dog in need,
She gave it a home, regardless of breed:
From Boxers to Terriers, Hounds to Dalmatians,
Spaniels to Labradors, Poodles to Alsatians.

The kennels proved quite a squeeze.
Some dogs preferred sleeping under the trees.
Dogs did what dogs do and multiplied until
The mansion house had an overspill!

Finding space suddenly became harder,
Even puppies were left in attics or the larder!
So many dogs appeared on the land,
Things soon started to get out of hand.

When hungry the dogs began to eat
A dead sheep placed in the kitchen.
The smell and flies rising from the floor
Also greeted visitors at the front door!

The Rolls Royce was deployed in relays,
With delighted dogs chauffeured every day.
Though locals declared it rather peculiar
For puppies to be born inside a 'Roller'.

Miss Pyne was seen cleaning the kennels
Dressed in a mink coat and cricket flannels.
But the dogs dominated her, of course,
Things were rapidly going from bad to worse.

Within months dogs roamed everywhere -
From bedroom to bathroom, kitchen to cellar!
Seventy dogs turned the mansion into a squat,
With a bold brigade of rampant rats.

The vet called at nine o'clock in the morning
And was still treating dogs late in the evening!
Their aches, anxieties and ailments,
Did not earn Miss Pyne any compliments.

Straight way the veteran vet could tell
This was not Dog Paradise but Dog Hell.
Miss Pyne completely failed to understand
That she had lost overall command.

In time dog numbers began to decline,
While Miss Pyne became unsound in mind.
As the mansion fell into disrepair,
The last dogs were taken into proper care.

Though kind to her pets all the time,
The responsibility lay with Miss Pyne.
Her dog mismanagement was sublime;
Which vets considered close to a crime.

Dogs require space to run around
And a home which is safe and sound,
With a feeding routine always on time.
Yet none of these applied to Miss Pyne !

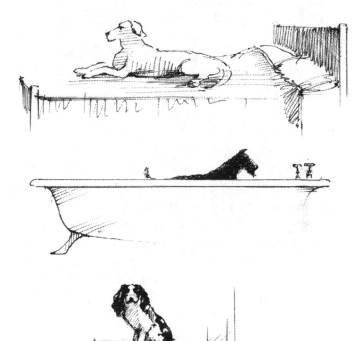

Duke Upsets Met !

Fame seemed assured, or so they thought,
For Duke, the Alsatian of Brixton Station:
The first employed dog of the Met.

Yet, despite being around, it was found,
Thefts from staff bags upwards crept.
Until detectives tracked down the culprit!

None other than Himself - Duke of the Met!
Who'd wait for staff to vacate their seats
Before nosing in bags for sandwiches or sweets!

His handler was stunned with grief -
The first Met dog was an opportunist thief!
Though his petty pilfering campaign proved brief.

So, after being caught Duke was put on report.
The rebuke to Duke made it crystal clear,
He'd soon better change his behavior !

Anymore illegal, in-house shopping
And Duke of the Met would be swapping
His street beat for the Charge Sheet!

Pekinese Pleases Peckish Pet Boa

From the cat flap squeezed Mitzi the Pekinese
And her slithering killer was equally pleased!
But a peckish pet boa constrictor
Is a most dangerous neighbour -
For she swallowed Mitzi with ecstatic ease!

P.S.
It truly came to pass.
Alas.

How to Break a Pit Bull Terrier's Grip

In Belo Horizonte, Brazil,
A pit bull terrier

bit
Gabriel Almeida, aged 11.

Did the boy scream ?
Did anyone try to rescue him ?

There was no need.
Gabriel drove off the pit bull

By biting it so hard,
he lost a tooth.

The Costliest Spaniel in Britain

Despite his five figure cost,
We do not believe it's money lost,
To maintain, restore and make well
George, our Cavalier King Charles Spaniel.

First night at home George cried in his bed
Loud enough to wake the dead,
Until he was laid on his mistress's duvet,
Where he's slept ever since, night and day!

George's coat has proved somewhat duff,
For its never lost its puppy fluff;
And so, missed the spaniel's traditional note,
Epitomized in a glossy, shimmering coat.

Our George collects aches and ailments,
From leg and hip complaints to obesity;
From vomiting to food allergies,
And sudden attacks of nervous anxiety!

But that's not all, so much more -
Suspected mange and serious skin strife,
Needing a shampoo bath twice a week,
And fortnightly serum shots all his life!

He's only got six gnashers left
For his chompers are prone to rotting.
Not that the dentist minds,
As he's the recipient of all the costing!

Even on a weekend holiday,
George brings bad luck straight away.
He bit a baited fish hook that made his lip pout
And, yet, another vet winkled it out!

What's more - and you'd never guess -
Following an attack by a Staffie,
George suffered post traumatic stress
Requiring a session with a dog therapist!

George also refuses to play games,
Eat doggy food or chase balls.
He can also be tyrannically rude
To boyfriends making home calls.

Further faults hear and see,
Such as his persistent snoring
Or licking body lotion off strangers' legs.
Provide proof George is never boring!

Yet George brings joy into our lives,
And with him happiness always survives.
He only asks for our affection
And, in return, offers total devotion.

Its not his fault he's usually ill
And needs another bandage or pill.
Just remember when we were low,
He made out eyes once more glow.

We don't care about the money
George shows us what's fun and funny.
He never does any harm
And is better than a burglar alarm.

So, just forget about George's costs,
We'll do whatever's required
For our little, family dog,
Who's beloved, adored and admired!

Toby and the Heimlich Manoeuvre

Debbie beat her chest as she choked
On a piece of apple lodged in her throat.

Toby, her two-year-old golden retriever,
Did not want to be without an owner.

So he pushed Debbie onto the ground,
Then jumped on her chest with a bound.

In order to help her breathing recover,
Toby copied her Heimlich Manoeuvre.

He certainly did his very, very best,
By jumping up and down on her chest.

The piece of fruit was soon dislodged,
And to properly finish the rescue job
Toby set about licking Debbie's face
To stop her passing out!

Without Toby's fast response,
Doctors declared,
Within minutes Debbie would have been dead

Piqued Peke

Pippa's beloved owners flew away
For a well-deserved fortnight's holiday.
But she sulked when they came home,
Preferring to be left strictly alone,
And in the same room refused to stay!

Pet Epic Trek

How on earth did Nicky know,
When and where to go?

Did she lock inbuilt radar
Onto some guiding star?

Without money or map
And vulnerable to 24-hour attack.

Yet, overcame so many trials
In an odyssey of 2,000 miles.

From beloved family dog to loner,
Lost in the desert of Southern Arizona.

Deserts are designed to slaughter,
Denying food, shade and water.

Yet, Nicky endured and survived.
Cacti shade, dew and grubs kept her alive.

Somehow she managed the heat.
One dog the sun could not beat.

Nor did Nicky wilt from the icy blow,
When starry nights fell below zero.

She not only endured the sun,
But somehow crossed the Grand Canyon.

Even now, we catch our breath,
Wondering how she survived such depths.

Whether a mile high or a mile low,
How did Nicky know where to go?

It seems beyond all reasonable truth.
Yet her survival is ample proof.

Sweet memories combatted hazards,
Raging rivers, howling blizzards.

Snow capped ranges and peaks,
Climbed and conquered over weeks.

Was she not nightly scared
Of slinking wolves or bounding bears?

Her intelligence, her greatest skill,
Prevented her from being killed.

Deserts, canyons, mountains, ice, snow;
Not one could deliver the killer blow.

Nicky showed qualities of canine character
That were endemic and enshrined in her:

Strength, commitment, shrewdness,
Belief, an inexhaustible doggedness.

And this driven, motivated Alsatian bitch,
Never once had a single hitch.

Did she ever suffer an attack
On what was always a perilous trek?

If she did, then she survived,
For she emerged triumphant and alive.

Two thousand miles she walked alone
And safely navigated herself home.

Did they gasp when Nicky reappeared?
No longer fatally lost as they had feared.

Southern Arizona to Selah, Washington -
The pet epic trek of an Alsatian heroine.

And what a welcome home she was given
On seeing the canine messiah re-arisen!

Snarler the Devourer

Snarler is the Supreme Devourer -
    A half cocker spaniel who'll not be beat
For being a dog who refuses any meat,
    But everything else just loves to eat!

He adores all kinds of shoes and duvets,
    Besides socks, knickers and tights.
And if that doesn't sound like food,
    He also consumes stacks of wood!

He eats paper tissues from the basket,
    And once devoured the kitchen mat.
While the fur he ate from his own tail
    Has no intention of ever growing back!

Snarler has tried to eat bathroom towels,
    But can find food almost anywhere.
When younger he ate his own collar,
    And the wooden arm of a rocking chair!

Snacks include nuggets of coal,
    Any kind of upholstery and braid,
While melons skins are swallowed whole
    And fresh newspapers daily devoured.

Visitors only seem to make matters worse,
    When Snarler extends his eating spree -
He likes tucking into strangers' coats
    And on their umbrellas prefers to wee !

Not content with a present or two
     On the morning of Xmas festivity,
Snarler celebrated by chewing up
     The beautifully decorated xmas tree!

Snarler resolutely refuses dog diets,
     So they're taking their cocker spaniel
To a warren of unsuspecting rabbits,
     Hoping they'll alter Snarler's eating habits !

Colour Clash

Trixie the fox terrier laid his weary head
On his beloved mistress's white satin bed,
But the mud and rain
Left quite a dark stain,
Though his mistress only saw bright red!

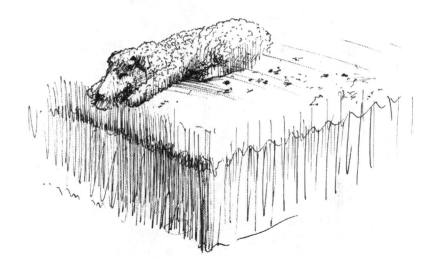

Brave, Blind Norman

A blind, homeless golden retriever
Will, surely, never be much of an achiever.

He lay day after day in the animal home,
Feeling so sad and so alone.

Who'd offer their love and home outright,
To a dog without any sight ?

But when Mandy and Mitch saw Norman,
He instantly won their love and attention !

They took Norman home and said,
He's the best dog we've ever had !

Though half blind he'd walk,
And follow the direction of any talk !

His personality was kind and warm
And his nature so gentle and calm.

He'd lay on the floor and let a friendly foot
Tickle his belly or softly touch his snout.

But Norman liked it best when set free
To run on the beach next to the sea !

No chair or table there to get in his way,
So he'd run about in joyous display !

Beside the sea Norman could run,
And show he was full of energy and fun !

Until, on one occasion, Norman stopped
And suddenly halted on the spot !

Norman looked around anxiously,
As he gazed blindly into the pounding sea !

Before his owners could stop Norman
Into the receding tide started to run !

Worse was soon too come,
As into the swirling sea Norman swam !

His owners began shouting and yelling,
For Blind Norman to stop swimming !

But on and on Norman swam,
To where a little girl was about to drown !

Though it might sound absurd,
Her screams for help only Norman heard !

He might have been blind as a bat,
But Norman's hearing had overcome that.

The girl hung onto Norman's neck,
Who turned and began the long swim back !

Norman heard his owners' calls to him,
And towards them began to swim.

The waves were high, the sea turned rough,
But Norman - tho' blind - was brave and tough !

The waves were higher than he'd ever known,
Yet Norman did not let the little girl drown !

He swam with all his strength and might,
As against the current he tried to fight.

He overcame the pounding, cruel sea
To finally reach the beach safely.

And, once, Norman's paws touched the shore,
He became the Local Dog Hero for evermore !

Song of the Homeless Mongrel

You won't find me at home,
    I've learnt how to live alone.
Homeless mongrels lie low,
    What have we got to show?

You won't find me in the day,
    I know its wiser to hide away.
I suppose I'm not very nice
    As I collect fleas and lice.

You won't see me on a lead
    Or having a decent daily feed.
At night I quietly creep about,
    And in bin bags shove my snout.

You won't hear me whimper,
    Whether its summer or winter.
Can't you see, can't you tell,
    I'm the homeless, ugly mongrel.

Of Wolf

Remember me.
I'll never be your guest.
I demand mountain,
River, valley, forest.

Remember me.
I'll never be led.
My howl is said
To disturb the dead.

Remember me.
I'm leader of the pack.
No one trusts me.
They believe I'll attack.

Remember me.
I'm loyal and true.
But never given
My worth and due.

Remember me.
I'm the one
From whom
Your beloved dog hails from.

References

BARBOU, Alfred. *Dogs We Love*
(Geneva: Minerva)

CLUTON-BROCK, Juliet. *Dog*
(London: Dorling Kindersley)

COOPER, Jilly. *Animals in War*
(London: William Heinemann)

COOPER, Jilly. *Intelligent and Loyal*
(London: Eyre Methuen)

COREN, Stanley & WALKER, Janet. *What Do Dogs Know*
(London: Simon and Schuster)

COREN, Stanley. *The Intelligence of Dogs*
(London: Headline)

CREW, Frank. *Devoted to Dogs*
(London: Frederick Muller)

ERWITT, Elliot. *Dog Dogs*
(London: Phaidon Press)

HADDON, Celia. *Faithful to the End*
(London: Headline)

HARRIS, Rolf. *True Animal Tales*
(London: Century)

KENNEDY, Sarah. *Terrible Pets*
(London: Penguin)

LEWIS, Martin. *Dogs in the News*
(London: Little Brown Books)

LLOYD JONES, Buster. *The Animals Came in One by One*
(London: Secker and Warburg)

MACDONOGH, Katharine. *Reigning Cats and Dogs*
(London: Fourth Estate)

MASSON, Jeffrey. *Dogs Never Lie About Love*
(London: Vintage)

MORRIS, Desmond. *Dogwatching*
(London: Jonathan Cape)

NEEDLES, Colleen & CARLSON, Kit. *Working Dogs*
(London: Discovery Books)

SIMONS, Paul. *Pet Heroes*
(London: Orion)

WHITFIELD, Kit. *Where Dogs Dream*
(London: MQP)